Using Simple Machines

Levers All Around

by Trudy Becker

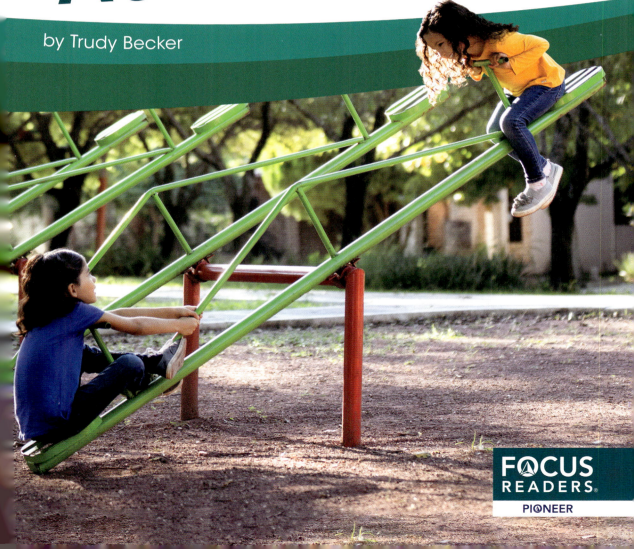

www.focusreaders.com

Copyright © 2024 by Focus Readers®, Lake Elmo, MN 55042. All rights reserved. No part of this book may be reproduced or utilized in any form or by any means without written permission from the publisher.

Focus Readers is distributed by North Star Editions:
sales@northstareditions.com | 888-417-0195

Produced for Focus Readers by Red Line Editorial.

Photographs ©: iStockphoto, cover, 1, 10; Shutterstock Images, 4, 6, 8, 12, 14 (top), 14 (bottom), 17, 18, 21

Library of Congress Cataloging-in-Publication Data
Names: Becker, Trudy, author.
Title: Levers all around / by Trudy Becker.
Description: Lake Elmo, MN : Focus Readers, [2024] | Series: Using simple machines | Cover title. | Includes bibliographical references and index. | Audience: Grades K-1
Identifiers: LCCN 2022058997 (print) | LCCN 2022058998 (ebook) | ISBN 9781637395981 (hardcover) | ISBN 9781637396551 (paperback) | ISBN 9781637397671 (ebook pdf) | ISBN 9781637397121 (hosted ebook)
Subjects: LCSH: Levers--Juvenile literature.
Classification: LCC TJ147 .B3825 2024 (print) | LCC TJ147 (ebook) | DDC 621.8--dc23/eng/20230103
LC record available at https://lccn.loc.gov/2022058997
LC ebook record available at https://lccn.loc.gov/2022058998

Printed in the United States of America
Mankato, MN
082023

About the Author

Trudy Becker lives in Minneapolis, Minnesota. She likes exploring new places and loves anything involving books.

Table of Contents

CHAPTER 1
Moving Up 5

CHAPTER 2
What Are Levers? 9

CHAPTER 3
Levers Everywhere 13

THAT'S AMAZING!
Catapults 16

CHAPTER 4
Fun with Levers 19

Focus on Levers • 22
Glossary • 23
To Learn More • 24
Index • 24

Chapter 1

Moving Up

A man sits on a seesaw outside. A girl comes over to him. She sits on the other end of the seesaw. The man is heavier than the girl. But he rises into the air.

The seesaw is a lever. Levers can help people move things. They make work easier. People don't need to use as much **effort**. Levers are one of the six **simple machines**.

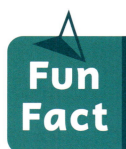

Fun Fact: Seesaws are not the only playground levers. Swings are levers, too.

Chapter 2

What Are Levers?

All simple machines help people do jobs. Levers are useful in many different ways. People use levers to lift **loads**. Levers also help people hit or break things. Levers can even help hold things together.

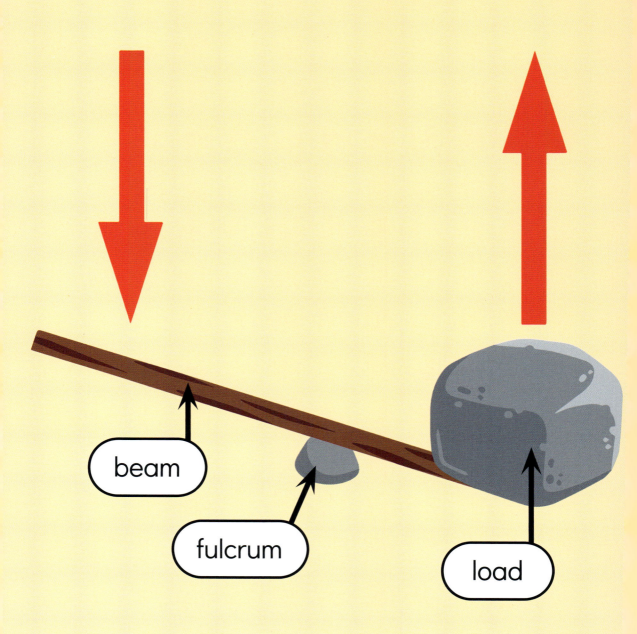

A lever has two main parts. There is a long **beam**. Then there is a **fulcrum**. That is where the beam moves. People add effort to the beam. That **force** helps move a load.

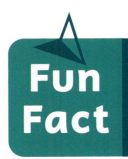
Fun Fact There are three kinds of levers. Each has the fulcrum in a different place.

Chapter 3

Levers Everywhere

People use levers every day. Tools like **pliers** are levers. So are many common school supplies. Scissors are levers. Staplers are levers, too.

Hammers and rakes are both levers. People hold these tools near the fulcrum at one end. They add effort in the middle. Then the other end moves. People can shift loads such as nails and leaves.

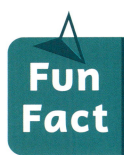

Levers can help people move heavy items.

That's Amazing!

Catapults

One kind of lever is a **catapult**. People can use catapults to throw heavy things. Long ago, people used catapults in wars. They put big stones on one end. They used effort to move the lever. Then the stones flew through the air.

Chapter 4

Fun with Levers

Levers are used for hard jobs. But levers are used for fun, too. Many games and sports use levers as **equipment**. Without levers, the games couldn't happen.

For example, baseball bats are levers. Players hold bats near the fulcrum. They add effort to swing. The balls are the loads. When players swing, the balls go flying.

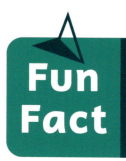

Fun Fact

Nutcrackers are levers, too. They help people crack nuts more easily.

FOCUS ON
Levers

Write your answers on a separate piece of paper.

1. Write a sentence that explains the main idea of Chapter 3.
2. What is the most helpful way you use levers in your life? Why?
3. How many kinds of levers are there?
   - A. ten
   - B. five
   - C. three
4. Where is the fulcrum on a pair of scissors?
   - A. in the finger holes on the handle
   - B. in the middle where the blades connect
   - C. at the bottom tip of the blade

Answer key on page 24.

Glossary

beam
A long, straight bar made of a hard material.

catapult
A machine that throws large objects.

effort
The force added to a lever.

equipment
Items needed to do something.

force
A push or pull that changes how something moves.

fulcrum
The point a lever balances on and where it moves.

loads
Objects that are lifted or moved.

pliers
Tools that people use to hold, twist, or cut things.

simple machines
Machines with only a few parts that make work easier.

To Learn More

BOOKS

Blevins, Wiley. *Let's Find Levers*. North Mankato, MN: Capstone Press, 2021.

Mattern, Joanne. *Levers*. Minneapolis: Bellwether Media, 2020.

NOTE TO EDUCATORS

Visit **www.focusreaders.com** to find lesson plans, activities, links, and other resources related to this title.

Index

B
beam, 10–11

C
catapults, 16

F
fulcrum, 10–11, 15, 20

S
seesaw, 5, 7

Answer Key: 1. Answers will vary; 2. Answers will vary; 3. C; 4. B